To

From

Date

A BRAVE BIG
SISTER

A BIBLE STORY ABOUT MIRIAM

RACHEL SPIER WEAVER ANNA HAGGARD

Illustrated by ERIC ELWELL

HARVEST Kids™

HARVEST HOUSE PUBLISHERS
EUGENE, OREGON

A Brave Big Sister

Text © 2017 by Rachel Spier Weaver and Anna Haggard
Artwork © 2017 by Eric Elwell

HARVEST KIDS is a registered trademark of The Hawkins Children's LLC. Harvest House Publishers, Inc., is the exclusive licensee of the federally registered trademark HARVEST KIDS.

Published by Harvest House Publishers
Eugene, Oregon 97402

www.harvesthousepublishers.com

ISBN 978-0-7369-7079-2 (pbk.)
ISBN 978-0-7369-7080-8 (eBook)

Cover and interior design by Left Coast Design

Published in association with the literary agency of Wolgemuth & Associates, Inc.

Printed in China

17 18 19 20 21 22 23 24 25 / LP / 10 9 8 7 6 5 4 3 2 1

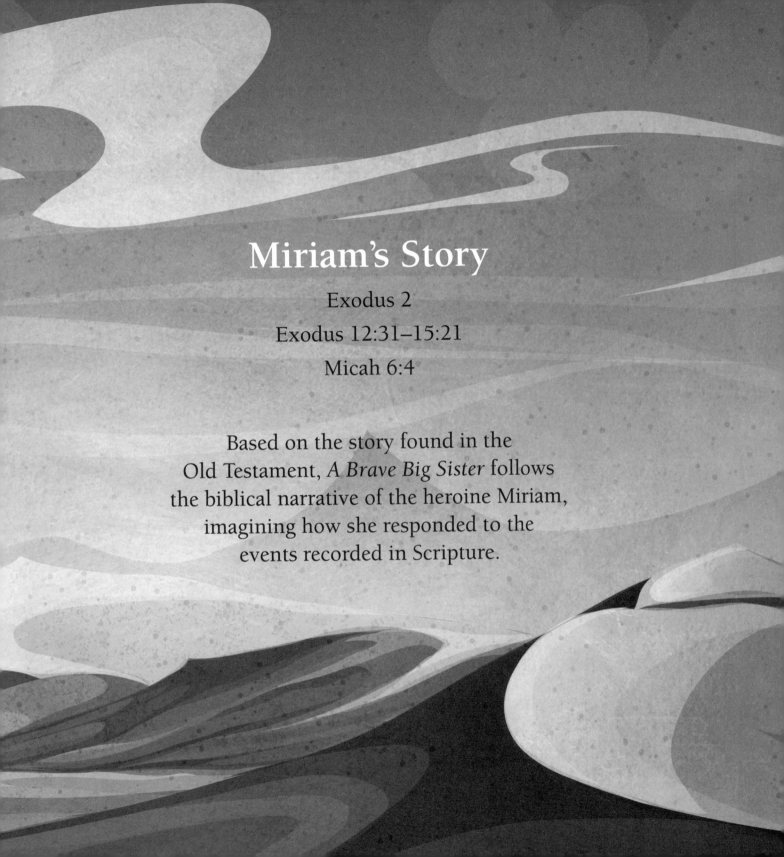

Miriam's Story

Exodus 2

Exodus 12:31–15:21

Micah 6:4

Based on the story found in the
Old Testament, *A Brave Big Sister* follows
the biblical narrative of the heroine Miriam,
imagining how she responded to the
events recorded in Scripture.

A baby!" squealed Miriam when Mom and Dad announced their family was adding a new member.

Soon Mom gave birth to a baby boy.

When Miriam saw him, she gasped. "He is the most beautiful baby!"

Her baby brother had huge, dark, intelligent eyes and a head of thick, black curls.

But Miriam's baby brother was not safe.

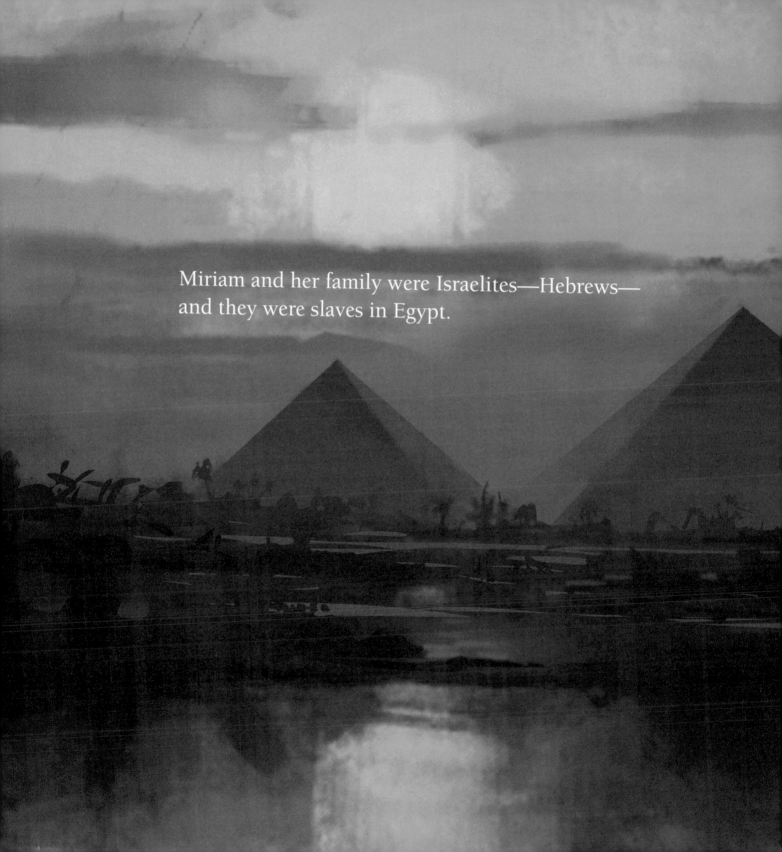

Miriam and her family were Israelites—Hebrews—
and they were slaves in Egypt.

Pharaoh, the king of Egypt, was afraid the Israelite slaves would take his place as king. So he declared to his people, "No more Israelite baby boys are allowed in my kingdom!"

For three months, Miriam, Mom, and Dad hid the new baby in their home.

When it became too dangerous for the baby to stay with them, Miriam's mom purchased a basket and covered it with tar and pitch to make it waterproof.

Early one morning, Miriam and her mom slipped out of the house and tiptoed through their neighborhood to the Nile River. Mom carried the baby close to her, and Miriam carried the special basket.

When they arrived at the Nile, Mom tucked the
sleeping baby in the basket and placed the basket
in the river.

With tears in her eyes, she said, "Miriam, will you watch your brother while I work?"

Miriam nodded. "I will, Mom."

As the morning sun rose over the water, Miriam's mother left. Miriam hid in the high grass, watching the basket, which was sheltered among the reeds at the river's edge.

"God, will you please protect our little baby?" Miriam prayed.

God loved Miriam, and God heard her prayer.

Hours passed. Miriam watched patiently.

But then Miriam heard laughter behind her. A princess—Pharaoh's daughter—was walking to the riverbank with her servants to bathe.

"Waaaaaa," Baby Brother wailed.

The princess stopped and saw the basket!

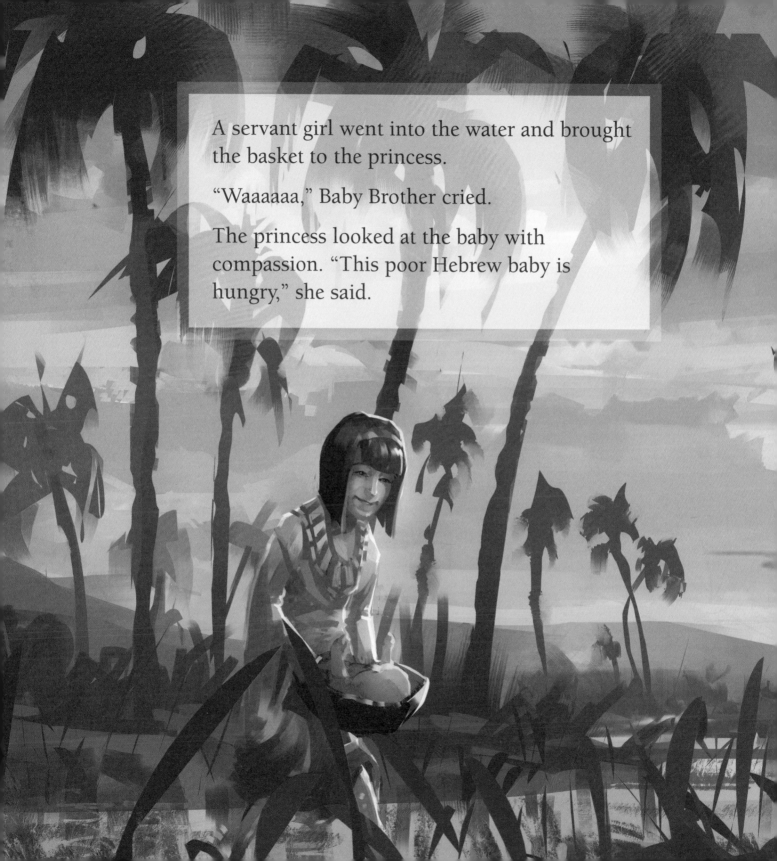

A servant girl went into the water and brought the basket to the princess.

"Waaaaaa," Baby Brother cried.

The princess looked at the baby with compassion. "This poor Hebrew baby is hungry," she said.

Miriam had to think quickly. Suddenly she had an idea, one that could save her brother's life.

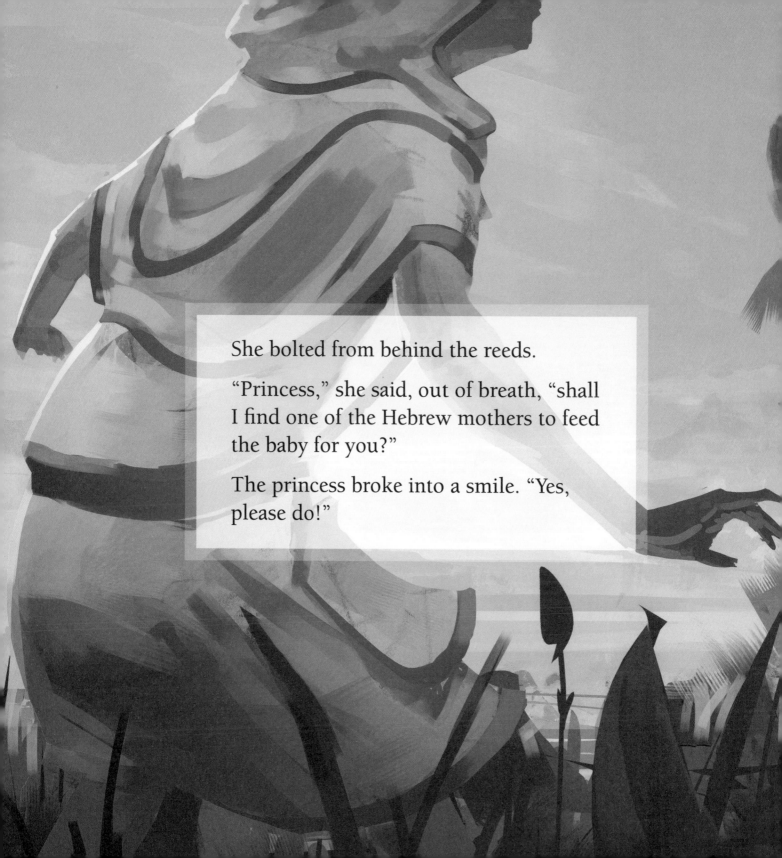

She bolted from behind the reeds.

"Princess," she said, out of breath, "shall I find one of the Hebrew mothers to feed the baby for you?"

The princess broke into a smile. "Yes, please do!"

Almost before the princess finished speaking, Miriam dashed off.

Darting through the tall grass, Miriam almost burst with joy from carrying a giant secret in her heart. She wasn't going to find just any mother to feed the baby.

"I am going to find the best mom of all—*my mom*."

When Miriam found her mother, she shouted, "Mom, Mom! Our baby is going to be safe—and *you* are going to take care of him!"

"*What?*" Mom sputtered in reply.

Before her mom could say anything more, Miriam grabbed her hand and ran straight to the princess.

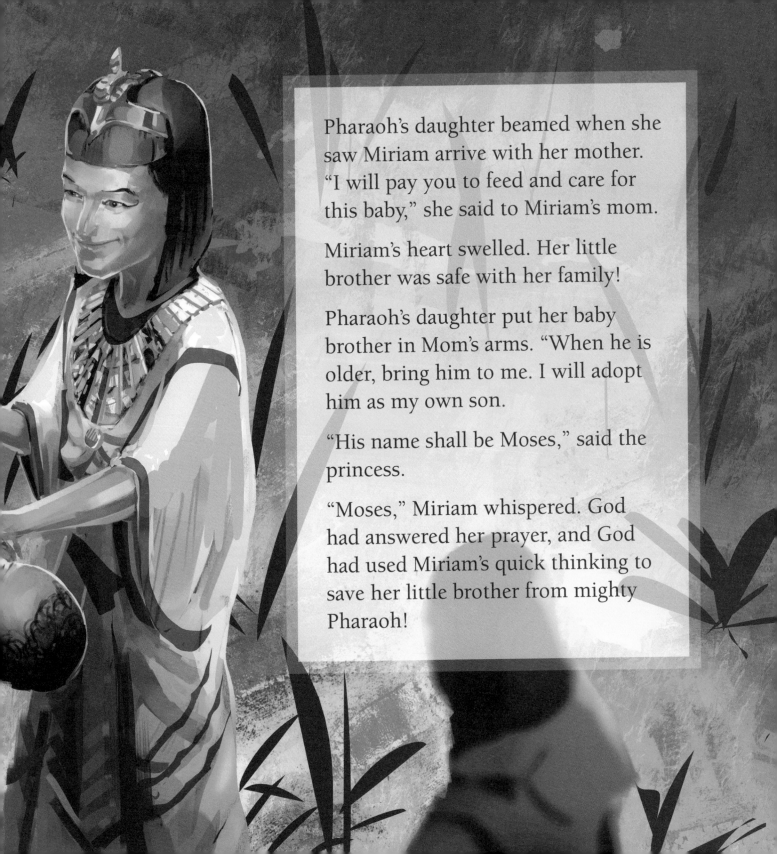

Pharaoh's daughter beamed when she saw Miriam arrive with her mother. "I will pay you to feed and care for this baby," she said to Miriam's mom.

Miriam's heart swelled. Her little brother was safe with her family!

Pharaoh's daughter put her baby brother in Mom's arms. "When he is older, bring him to me. I will adopt him as my own son.

"His name shall be Moses," said the princess.

"Moses," Miriam whispered. God had answered her prayer, and God had used Miriam's quick thinking to save her little brother from mighty Pharaoh!

When Miriam and Moses grew up, God chose them and their brother Aaron to lead the Hebrew people out of slavery. God equipped Miriam with a beautiful voice to sing and to speak up for her people as a prophet.

And God asked Moses to lead the people from Egypt, away from Pharaoh.

With God's guidance, Miriam, Moses, and the other Israelites fled Egypt—all the way to the Red Sea.

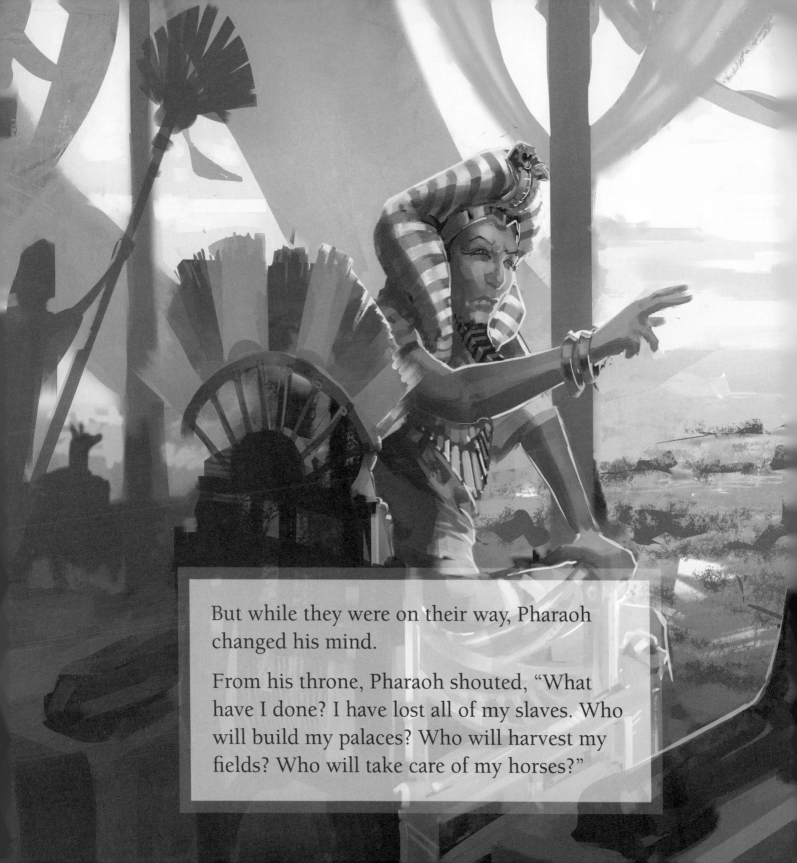

But while they were on their way, Pharaoh changed his mind.

From his throne, Pharaoh shouted, "What have I done? I have lost all of my slaves. Who will build my palaces? Who will harvest my fields? Who will take care of my horses?"

So he ordered his military officers to ready his great army of chariots.

"We will return the Hebrew slaves to Egypt," Pharaoh said as he led his fierce army through the desert in pursuit of the Israelites.

That evening, Miriam looked across the path the Israelites had followed. She saw the approaching army. "Moses, it's Pharaoh!" she cried.

Before her were the crystal blue waters of the Red Sea. Behind her was Pharaoh leading his mighty army of chariots.

"We are trapped!"

Miriam prayed, "God, you saved Moses from Pharaoh when he was a little baby—you can do anything! Please rescue us from Pharaoh again."

God said, "Moses, raise your staff over the sea."

Moses raised his shepherd's staff before the sea. A strong wind blew toward the sea, making a path between the waters.

Miriam, Moses, and all the Israelites walked between two walls of water.

The wind roared as it held the water in place. The air smelled like salt and fish.

Under her feet, Miriam felt dry sand.

After hours of walking, Miriam and all the
Israelites stepped from the Red Sea into the desert.

Moses lifted his staff over the water. The walls of water crashed together, covering the path of the Israelites! God had protected the Israelites, and Pharaoh's army had been swallowed by the sea.

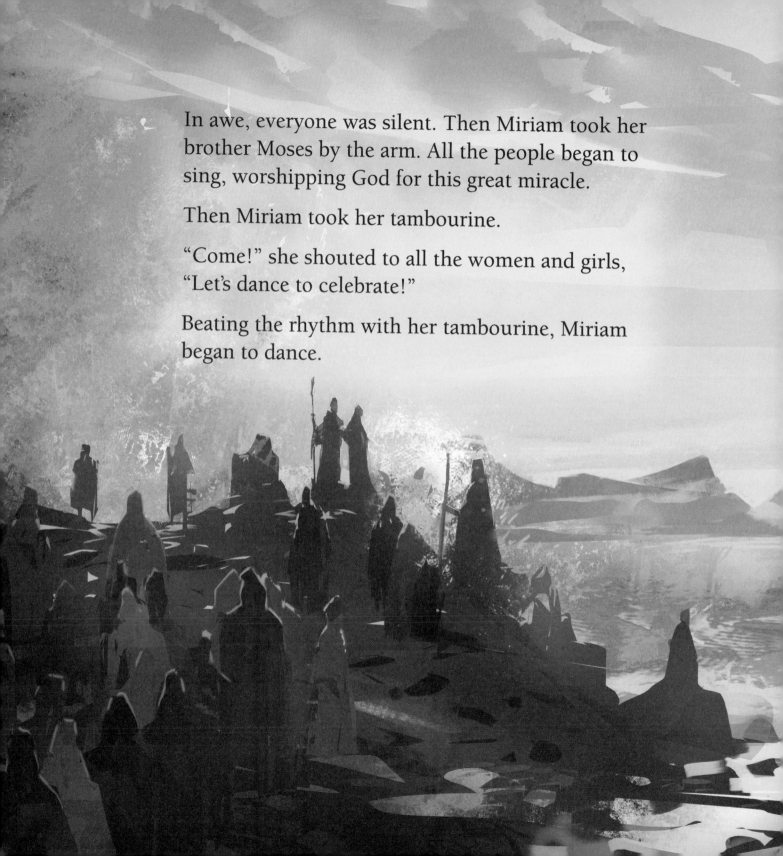

In awe, everyone was silent. Then Miriam took her brother Moses by the arm. All the people began to sing, worshipping God for this great miracle.

Then Miriam took her tambourine.

"Come!" she shouted to all the women and girls, "Let's dance to celebrate!"

Beating the rhythm with her tambourine, Miriam began to dance.

Her tambourine sounded, rrring-jingle-jangle-rrring.

Following Miriam's lead, hundreds of thousands of girls and women began to play their tambourines together, quietly at first:

rrring-jingle-jangle-chaa-chacha-rring…

And then louder and faster…RRING-jingle-jangle-chaa-chacha-RRING!

The girls and women danced with Miriam. The desert echoed with music.

What a great, noisy party the Israelites had that day! Before the assembly, Miriam belted out a song to God:

Sing to God—what a victory!

The horse and rider fell into the sea!

Miriam praised God, who had given her the courage to save her little brother Moses and who had performed mighty miracles so his special people could be free.

· REFLECTION QUESTIONS ·

- How did God use Miriam to help Moses when he was a baby?

- Miriam helped her mother by keeping her brother safe and then calling her mom when the princess needed someone to care for the baby. When we help others, we serve God. In what ways have you helped someone in your family?

- As Miriam grew, she became a leader in her community. Can you think of other women who are leaders like Miriam?

Dear reader,

What Bible stories captured your attention as a child? The stories dramatized on Sunday school felt boards often featured Noah and his ark, David and Goliath, and Paul traveling on his missionary journeys. And rightly so! These stories depict giants of our faith. But the Bible also elevates women—faith-filled adventurers who lead, make brave decisions, and risk everything to follow God. Called and Courageous Girls is a series of children's books that star gutsy biblical women who unleash the kingdom of God.

We are thrilled that you have chosen to read this book in the Called and Courageous Girls series. Our prayer is that these books will provide hours of enjoyable reading, prompt engaging and challenging conversations, and inspire your children to use their talents, passions, and gifts for the kingdom.

Blessings,

Rachel and Anna